OUR DADDY
THE TREE CLIMBER

Sell your books at sellbackyourBook.com!
Go to sellbackyourBook.com and get an instant price quote. We even pay the shipping - see what your old books are worth today!

Inspected By: Wilson_Chub1

00061282535

0006128 **2535** S

00061282535

Dedication

To my husband Price. We are so grateful for always going above and beyond. We love you.

To our Daddy, the Tree Climber. Love, Elijah, Isabella, and Joshua

Special thank you to Brittney, who made my first book possible with your incredible designs.

Sometimes there is rain and you still wake up and go outside.

Daddy, Sissy and I watch you go to work and we cry because we want to come with you.

We miss you Daddy! When I grow up, I want to be just like you!

You climb BIG trees and
one day I want to go up
there too.

"Someday when you get big," you say.

But I want to grow up
NOW.... It is not fair! I do not
want to be little.

Not fair!

We hear a big loud truck and Sissy and I both yell, "Daddy is home! Daddy is home!"

We giggle and both run our way to the door. Finally, you are home!

You walk in the house and say right away, "My babies! My babies! Oh, how I missed my babies!"

We missed you too Daddy!
All day long!

Your clothes are SO yucky
Daddy! It is time for your
bath!

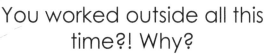
You worked outside all this time?! Why?

"To buy you all toys, food,
and your brother diapers"
you say. But oh, how excited
we are to play.

Let's play!

"ROOOAAR!" You yell, as
you chase us around.

Sissy and I run SO fast and try to hide from you Daddy.

You follow behind us saying,
"I am the tickle monster!
ROAAAR!"

Sissy and I are laughing so hard!

"AAAHHHH!" We yell! You
found us! You found us!
And now you are tickling us
away.

My Daddy is a tree climber.

And one day, when I am not little anymore, I will be one too.

About the Author

Erika Pitstick is the proud mother of three, Elijah, Isabella and Joshua. She is married to Price who has a tree service company. Erika loves to help with the company, but is also very passionate about finding new ways to connect with her family. She loves to cook, write and film/edit videos.

CPSIA information can be obtained
at www.ICGtesting.com
Printed in the USA
LVHW071426181119
637665LV00005B/1446/P